BLACK & WHITE

DOMINIQUE SWEAT

BLACK & WHITE

CONTENTS

For *the people who have a hard time in the gray area and live in black and white*

Dedicated To - *The people who have helped me to see the world in color*

INTRODUCTION

There's something so beautiful and so isolating about being two or more things at once. Most of it is out of my control. I was born both Black and White. I was born both rich and poor. I was born with an attraction to both men and women. Then there are the beautiful isolations that I had created myself. I am both logical and emotional. I am both empathetic and detached. I am both deserted and surrounded. I am both fearful and fearless. When I realized that I could go on forever about polarities and navigating these complexities, I began to write.

SELF & OTHER

Dance With Me

Is my face too grave?
How should it be?
Everyone knows my wisdom
is not only in my teeth.

Don't be scared to be
your lesser self
You can call me baby
and I'll call you out.

It's not a coincidence
that you feel at home
That is how they all feel
when they lie with my bones.

Come and dance with me
and you'll leave when you're done.

The Twelfth House

I spend a lot of time here.
On a different spiritual plane
Somewhere between the past and future,
But not to be confused with the present.

With Saturn and Jupiter spinning
I have divine protection, but
It comes at a cost, a great one.
For there will always be loneliness.

Routine

To leave the oven and step into the cold
Pearly whites if the breakfast stays down
The loudest silence you've ever heard

Responsibilities await!
Fragmented organs will not excuse you
Answer the call and lose your mind

Opiate remedies and loose clothes
Burning red in a sea of blue
It's nothing new, it's nothing new

Treadmill treaties and pilate princess
Salt tunnels on cheeks in the car
Metal turns and lights come on

Fabricate a meal for the bin
The TV is on, music is playing, handheld distractions
Fatigue does not come to the rescue

Preheat the oven, the rotisserie
The north loop is about to begin
The loudest silence you've ever heard.

Making Adjustments

"What are you adjusting to?"

The world needs to adjust to me
My mere existence is a burden to the masses
The world doesn't see it that way

Brainwashed and simple-minded
Returning to a time where I am repressed
The world doesn't see it that way

Session after session, pill after pill
An epidemic of loneliness and dejection
The world doesn't see it that way

Substituting humans, moving faster and faster
Phony, conceited, with no ability to look inside
The world doesn't see it that way

Promising young women, maximal beauty
Melting pots, mixing knives, making men
That, that is how the world sees it

Try Harder

Is it because I am the middle child?
I must not have felt loved
In the way I needed to be loved

Is it because I am neither white nor black?
I must not have fit in
The way I should have fit in

Is it because I love women in that way?
I must have issues
In the way of valuing a man

Falling Lane

That doesn't raise a flag?
Or did you choose to ignore them like I did?

The reputation is earned and assigned
It's not made up or to be tested, or proven wrong

Young soldiers in the field are being bombed
And falling for it on Falling Lane

You're not the first tenant to make it to the house
Or the couch, the shower, and the new build

Pictures in wallets and 2 dozen red roses

All Too Well

Anger creeps into my jaw
It rests in my bones and
It represses my despair

Parental Guidance

Two water signs trine another
The circle was completed and depleted
Losing the metasoma didn't hurt the megalopa
At least that's what it thought

The fish circled every aspect
Deep, shallow, sky lines, and swamps
Crustaceans scoured shorelines alone
Telling the fish to keep swimming

The Chesapeake blue drowned
Waves crashed, and the earth faltered

Mercifully Medicated

Sleep, weep, sleep
Insomnia or drowsiness
To the nth degree

Creativity strikes to be
met with a dull out of
body experience

Pain is subdued but
please forget who you
were before all of this

The mirror won't remind you
when the eyes can't find you.

Satisfaction

Both a man and a woman
have grown languid
against my fingertips

My innocence still intact
as there was never such
a pleasure for me

Yet I crave the touch,
to be known from the
inside and the out

2000-D

Modern, shiny, and abundant
Only worthy in mint condition
The circulation brings the value
of this coin to face

The American explorer sets out again
Originality and luster supreme
The classics couldn't care less as
their patina gathers

Minted in the cold,
bearing a Northern attitude
The millennium grew unimportant
living free or dying in Jamestown.

Clear as Day

Millions awake in the middle of the night
A pit in your stomach, a scream in your throat
The crushing feeling and continuing on

The majority of the common do not care
A ballot to them, a bullet to us
It won't be that bad, spare the drama

Hand off the bible, surrounded by religious fanatics
But the rules don't apply to you
Roman salutes-
Oh, our hearts went out

Our hearts leapt from our chests as
history repeats itself, and you all did
nothing, said nothing.

Transients

For those who do not know how to be alone,
Leave the ones who do.

Actions of codependency and insecurity
Waiting is an inappropriate word

There is no acceptable amount of time
When such intimacy and love are shared

The loner will yearn for the lost future,
That has been promised to someone new

No grief will be felt as the love travels
To different shores before the sand is dry.

Do Better

Is it harder to be kind
To be real, meaningful
The world has shown
It's easy to be cruel

Adam's Rib

Pastel pastries and flowers
Divine dresses and feelings
Natal nurturers and empathy
Simple softness and beauty
Brilliant brains and loyalty
Luscious lovers and bravery

Iron Deficiency

Not strong enough to self-harm,
Or am I too strong to self-harm?
Or maybe I partake in self-harm every day.

I am a giver, through and through
My dreams of being selfish are hard to make a reality.

No one is at fault for the bruises on my skin
Or the heaviness in my heart.
Well, the fault belongs to a poor diet and anemia.

Princess Alexandrina

No, darlin'
I don't want to buy you bigger shoes
Or see you in a satin slip dress

Just twirl around in circles
and beg me to carry you up the stairs
I'll make the same jokes and
always pretend that yours are funny

You can paint my face
and I'll paint your nails
Swimming as mermaids
and sharing sugary treats

We'll have sweet tea summers
and build sand castles
surrounded by crabs and shells

When it's time to go to bed,
we can hide under the covers
and share secrets in our sleep
Yours are my favorite to keep

The Long Trail

I do not want to climb this mountain.
The journey has not been easy
and there are far more lows than highs.

But I will keep climbing this mountain
until I like the view.

To Be Loved, Is To Be Known

I don't crave love,
but I want to be known.
I want to be completely
understood and embraced.

I don't want to drink
I don't want to smoke
I don't want to fall in love,
get money, and move to the next.

Understand me. Feel me. Need me.
You can even hate me, but please
At least know who I truly am.

Kindred Notion

I was not touched when I was touched
I was scared and angry and confused
These feelings continue to appear
as I am touched in different places
by different people, at different times.

BLACK & WHITE

———————————

––––––––––––––––––––

The Dance

March with us, my dear.
For if you do not march,
You are not one of us

Sit with us, my soldier.
For you and your ancestors
To receive a salaried rest

Divine Diversity

I do not burn
in the presence
of the sun

My eyes can take
in so much light
and see in the dark

Exotic and unique
with desirable teeth,
brains and beauty

A shoo-in for
an open spot
on any team

Black and white,
sometimes gray.

Just a Quick Visit

Thirty-dollar co-pay, please
Are you ill
Mentally, physically, emotionally
I have just the thing!

Powder, powder blue
It's the thing for you!

Thirty-dollar co-pay, please
What do you want to talk about today
Work, relationships, purpose
See you next week!

Journaling and meditation
That'll do!

Thirty-dollar co-pay, please
Have you tried-
Working out, eating better, gratitude
Download this app!

She didn't get better
One more appointment!

Thirty-dollar co-pay please
This might hurt a little bit, ready?
Shock, pulse, inject
All better!

Insurance policies have changed
Fifty-dollar co-pay, please

Bad Vegetarian

I can't eat that
I don't want to eat that.
So, I said no.

I said no,
and you heard now.

My curiosity got the better of me,
and the goat tasted so good
But the illness it caused
nearly killed me

Black and White

Relax
       Cut
              Burn
It will never be straight enough

Learn
       Speak
              Act
It will never be good enough

Change
       Embrace
              Embody
It will never be real enough

Wake Up!

We've been here before
This show is on repeat

I don't even cry at it anymore
I don't even flinch

Does anyone really enjoy
a movie marathon?

I, for one, would like to
try something new.

Welcome to America

It must be nice to be that selfish
No one to reprimand you, and
why would they when you've
accomplished what they
could only dream of back home.
Your footprints go undetected.

Pack It Up

She would have never done that
If she loved you

He would still be here
If he wanted you

They wouldn't be there
If they barred you

I would have stayed
If I needed you

"You Should Model"

Skinny and symmetrical
    Or of black and white color

Smart and seductive
    Or of tongue and brain power

Athletic and aesthetic
    Or of beauty and bone structure

Noir

The harsh contrast
Highlights and dark
shadow space

Chalkboard drawings
Or Sharpie secrets
Adjust the vibrance

No warm tones
or cool sliders
needed now or ever

Greed

There is not much time left
Pick one that will stay when you can't,
and the silt hardens in the channel

What It All Comes Down To

The newborn baby will cry
as teardrops fall from her eyes

A man will never love you
the way a woman can

They steal, lie, cheat, and leave
and never wear their heart on their sleeve

No one wants to hear "not all men."
It's far too many for women not to adapt

A ritual of humiliation and despair
after believing "this one is different"

Not So Beautiful

The agents want me, interview me
Validation of my physical appearance

Friends, peers, and family insist that their lives
are better with me in it, lighter

Borderline underweight with visible abdominal muscles
and a clean bill of health, no due date on life

No financial burden or loans to repay,
There is no debt or surprises, responsible

Yet, I find myself undesirable
In a dark peace with an excruciating silence, sad.

You can say it to me all you want
but don't expect me to feel any different.

Buproprion Baby

The world lacks color
And the food is tasteless

I only order water now
When I go out to eat

Crossing things off my
Bucket list with no satisfaction.

Everyone disgusts me
Including the reflected stranger

This isn't the first time,
and it probably won't be the last.

The Natural Satellite

The *New Moon* is upon us,
Manifest, manifest, manifest
Journal, pen to paper

Squint for the *Waxing Crescent*
Take action and create
The tarot cards don't lie

First Quarter creeps in
Priorities and authorities
The witches will not rise

The *Waxing Gibbous* haunts us
Storms are brewing, a culmination
No one is coming to save you

Finally, the *Full Moon*
Charge your crystals, feel it all
Feel some more and cry

Waning Gibbous pushes rest
Take it easy and recover
Did you learn anything?

9 on the clock, *Third Quarter*
Time to let go, forgiveness
Meditation and contemplation

Waning Gibbous to complete the cycle
Burn the papers, fire and flames
Cleanse your being with gratitude

Gray Area

The sun is hot, that's a fact
When water turns to ice,
It's obviously cold

Night is dark,
It's more difficult to see
Wait until daylight

Yes, green means go
No, stop.

Expended and worn, used
Fresh and never before seen,
New

Ebony darkness, black
Blinding and milky, white

Now tell me,
How did it end?

I Can't Believe I'm Writing This Down

I don't want to go to the beach
Because that means my skin will darken.

I mostly mingle outside of color,
So I don't have to bear witness.

I feel disappointment constantly,
Don't tarnish our reputation further

I pick up on the disrespect, and
I need to call it what it is.

I Do Not Know

Is there a greater lesson to be learned here?
So many questions will go unanswered, and I feel
like a child learning the word "why" and testing it out.

A naive child that doesn't understand the tired
guardian saying something as simple as I don't know.
Not every question is meant to be answered.

To that, I ask why? Again, embracing the child.
Feelings and emotions are explainable, and I
refuse to believe that there's no logic to pain.

Black Truths

They do not love you.

It's not complicated.

Fraudulent

I do not know how to care for my hair.
I can't braid, I can't sew, I can't upkeep.
Even my mother knows how to do that.

I do not know how to display my anger.
I can't yell, I can't scream, I can't fight.
Even the white boy knows how to do that.

I do not know how to cook a nice meal.
I can't smoke, I can't fry, I can't season.
Even the tradwife knows how to do that.

I do not know how to leave it alone.
I can't ignore, I can't forget, I can't exist.
Even my father knows how to do that.

LOVE & HEARTBREAK

———————————

For However Long We Have

It begins with admiration, later becoming adoration
Predators follow with shiny glass chambers
The white dove, feeling safe, searches for a place to perch
Confined and dancing on the bell jar base
Lifting the glass, one final molting before the dove dies

I Knew You, and I Still Loved You

The smell of your sheets
and the day your parents were born

The way you take your coffee
and the name of your first love

The signature on the titles to your cars
and the day your second wife filed for divorce

The taste of your skin in the sun
and the secrets you buried in plain sight

The backseat of the green bug
and your father's dying words

The 5 am descent to the first floor
and your inability to express how you feel

The cost of your capital
and the bike accident scar

The stitches I removed from your head
And the fears that agonized you

I know if I asked you the names
of my siblings, nothing would come out

Making Sense of it All

Clearly, my looks were never
the problem. I don't think it
was my personality either.
It must have been something I said.
God knows, it was nothing I did.

Temporary Bliss

Foreheads pressed together
Warm breaths on lips
Pulled towards one another

Diving in the deep end
Making love in the shallows
Two creatures of water

Staring into the fireplace
Soft bodies intertwined
Falling into forever

Early Education

Does a mother have a favorite child?
Apples to oranges
Breasts to beasts

Soft, sweet, and deep
Landing on a cloud
My mane grew against your knife

Doubts evolved, but my loyalty
is like a drunk to a dive bar,
yours like a workaholic father

I don't wish you rain or winter
but I hope no one is around
when the tree falls in the forest.

Unlucky Break

Perhaps I had stayed too long
Like an in-law or an abused child
The dinner never got cold and
The conversation wasn't tiring
But it never felt like forever, the good kind.

It felt like the forever when you're waiting to
get the text that their plane landed or
a jail sentence for a crime you didn't commit

Love was there, sure
But the love never should have
made me shrink and shriek,
spiraling and self-loathing

Shock and betrayal hurt,
But it gave me closure that I didn't
need to beg for, it was edible and
easy to swallow after a couple of months

It still lives in the lining of my
stomach, and I can recall every
detail of the digestion.

Venusian Slip

I didn't need proof, nor
evidence to show,
but I collected it anyway

Driving in the rain
with no other lights around
just gas and golden arches

It's funny how the denial
becomes pleading and
emotional warfare

But I still sat on the sofa
and paid the kind lady
for her to say that you're wrong

Empathy got the best of me
Family, fireworks, and the need
to prove you still want me

The candles were blown out and
I was finally clear and clean, which
you couldn't understand

Circling and stealing
any moments you can
While the bed's still unmade

But it's okay because
the ring is still on your
finger, no?

Nai, Moro Mou

Your girl is gorgeous
Good morning, beautiful
I get nervous around you,
and I feel like a kid again.

Exotic and magnetic,
You pull me in, and I
can't keep my hands
or my eyes off of you.

You're perfect, don't
ever change a thing
Do you hear me?
I mean it. You're perfect.

My mind is calm around
you, everything is so
peaceful and quiet. Please
don't go, grab a T-shirt.

I want you. I need to
see you- we just spent
4 whole days together,
and I miss you already.

Why are you so good to me?
You are the best thing that
has ever happened to me.
Mine, Mine, Mine.

Which way should the
bedroom window face in
our house? Let's go see where
the sun sets on our dock.

Be patient with me, work
gets a little crazy. I can
lose track of time, but I
still need you and want you.

You're so good to me, and
the kids love you so much.
Winter me is so different,
just wait until summertime.

You looked so beautiful in
your little white dress today.
I am so lucky, thank you, and
I know I don't say it enough.

Meet me at the lot
It will only be a few minutes
I will try to do better.
It was probably a sunset.

I can't keep torturing you.
I can see it on your face,
and you won't admit it
but you will grow to resent me.

No, I do love you.
Let's talk in a few days.

And the Livin' is Easy

Is your skin burning
now that the days
are getting longer

Does her blonde hair
and youthful skin repulse you
as the breeze warms

The sound of boats on the
water and the sight of
daffodils warning you

It's time to let her go
and seek out another

Because I Used to Love It

I hate that the days are getting warmer
The sun is out longer and smoother waters
I hate that car doors are closing and
girls get out of them in crop tops and mini skirts

I hate that skinny dipping is a painful memory
And no longer a thrilling adventure
I hate when men call me beautiful and
The barista knows how to make a drink

I hate when friends want to order pizza
Or are impressed when I speak a new language
I hate that walking over the bridge is less
intriguing than trying to jump off of it

But most of all, I hate that I didn't listen
to my intuition and remember the rules.

Tomato, Tomato

Was any of it real?
You only used me to heal.

Your father died in June
And I pulled you out of the ruin.

I tried to tell you no
that I really should go

You felt safe in my arms
yet caused me so much harm

I know I will be okay
As long as this doesn't stay.

My intentions were kind and clear
You will be filled with regret and fear.

1100

Seven minutes in heaven could not have
prepared me for that moment
You left before I could leave you—

I gave you time to gather your thoughts
Talk to me.

Your actions have always been louder than your words

Red Sky at Night

The waves crashed into me, and I succumbed to the current
The sky was maroon as the sun came up, sirens screamed
I took warning, and the MOB alarm still rang loudly as
my sorrowful soul took the plunge into the tide

The water wasn't cold like I thought it would be
In fact, it lifted me up, and I was floating
Salt kissed my skin and drowned out my thoughts

I belonged and happily sank with the mermaids
Ignoring the seaweed that brushed my ankles
I trusted that the sea knew better and had years worth of
experience pulling victims and lovers overboard

Once my body absorbed and gave way,
the main grew tired and washed me to the shore
Shaken and cold, alone on a deserted island
I watched as the sea swallowed the next lass

It Does Not Matter

But you asked me out
and continued to chase me,
Begging for our lips to touch

But you said that I was
"the best thing that's ever happened"
to you, with tears in your eyes

But our signs matched
Our Venuses, our suns
Everything was aligned

But your son fell asleep in my arms
and your daughter and I
held one another, crying
knowing neither of us had your attention

But you moved on in a fortnight
And I'm completely lost while writing poetry.
A pile of loose jeans is growing on the floor.

Gut Feelings

Put me in a white jacket
in your mind, I do not care.

Just know that the satisfaction
Isn't yours to hold onto

I did what I did knowing
that you would do what you do.

I will not forgive myself for
believing things would be different

Remember that I do not forget
and may the widow rest in your walls.

Bloody Top Lip

The same wound reopens
But different blood bleeds
It's rare and red but limited

No amount of Aquaphor or
a homemade remedy will stop
the chapped skin from bleeding.

Physical wounds are still
easier to tend to than
the gaping hole in my heart

Filoi Sou

Bare legs on the pavement
Blurred vision and semi-catatonic
Less than a mile from your shores
What did you tell Lacy and Rick?

The build was done
And family wasn't scary
Lost a pretty penny
But did you tell Uncle Jerry?

You didn't have to sleep
With Jim's lousy bride
He supported your product
And yet you two still hide

Geoff wasn't surprised
When the blonde came around
The same precise age as me
No mystery to be found

No Surprise

I could have written this,
The end was inevitable.
Yet this band-aid has been
stuck for a year and almost
more painful to peel than the
pathetic day it was applied.

Loved, Past Tense

Did you even love me?

The nerves you felt talking to me
And the good impression you had to make

The drives you made past my windows
and unnecessary conversation starters

The forehead kisses, and the tears forming
In your eyes when I became a morning person

The awe you got when I finished your sentences
And the shock when I remembered every detail

The way your body trembled under my touch
And the warmth in the sheets we shared in the dark

The pride you felt in showing me off to your friends
And the whines you carried when I left your arms

The fancy, overpriced dinners we couldn't finish
because we needed to save room for one another

The way you ran when you thought I would first
And the shame you felt when it all ended

Of course I did.

Alpha, Beta, Gamma–

As I sit here in concourse A, I imagine you in concourse B
In your travel jeans and a shirt that has grown tight.

You have a twenty-something figurine whose heart is still in one piece,
or an older man cheating on his ailing wife by your side.

You're headed somewhere warm because you weren't built for the cold,
And leaving where you're needed most is what you do best.

It's a red eye to Atlanta, and no one can make you an iced cap-
puccino,
and your virtual assistant won't answer your questions about the
weather and tides.

You're always slightly nervous about your flights because your mother
has instilled it, but I can only hope that my plane bursts
into flames. Yours can land safely, somewhere warm.

Moon Illusion

She did not stand far behind, and many phases had cycled through

It took all of 11 minutes after the 11 months for me to fall apart.

There was nothing wrong with her, and she was quite pretty.

I didn't miss you. But the negative end was stronger than I thought.

Have I changed, or was the fruit unripe?

Dwell

Is it because I had half a decade with you
Or because there was another involved

Maybe I did not like who I was around you
Or the way you wanted us to live our lives

I know I loved you and cared for you
But those feelings turned a deep blue

I was able to quickly move on from you
But I didn't get so lucky the second time

Everything to Regret

Disturbing and painfully predictable
Taking advantage of my heartbreak
And throwing me into your life

My face contorts with a
mouth full of limes, and your face
kisses her with a mouth full of lies

At least I'm a twenty-something
and not a middle-aged maroon
dating girls without a developed cortex

They all understand my youthful mistakes
But they whisper about your callous blunders
And roll their eyes at the repeat offenses

A Mink Fur Coat in June

It's astronomy to a sea angel,
Truly, no subject for the spotlight.
Hand is still burning from the
stove and the lack of a fight.

There is no wine-stained dress
or pictures to touch the flame.
Just the occasional Russian
run-in to prove I was sane.

It was a game of checkers
all along, and I prefer my
games in black and white.
Red was never in our sight

Retrograde

An apology wouldn't do, and
my reputation will not
succumb to feverish forgiveness

Yet I would drain my entire being
To have another conversation-
It can't possibly end the same way

The equivalent of opening a tin can
and then dragging my tongue along
the bladed edge in hopes of resealing it

Must it be so easy for you
When I know that I am not at a loss
And your end is approaching

All four seasons have come and gone
And yet I haven't moved with them.
The longest day of the year.

Little Lamb

She follows, and she follows through.
A warm, white fleece.
Feeling for the keratin-wrapped bones
that I've been warned about,
But I have only found her laugh
as we play, tethered to one another.
I'm charmed to be Mary.

PAST & FUTURE

Old Soul

Was I too young when you
Expected me to lead my peers

Was I too young when you
Became a parent and got married

Was I too young when you
Kissed my collarbone and breasts

Was I too young when you
Placed my hand along your body

Was I too young when you
Gave me the job and flew me out

Was I too young when you
Left.

You Gave Me Life

Call me the Artful Dodger
I'll dance and sing until your
heart is crimson and full

Realistically, I could stay still
and he would put me on a
pedestal and praise the life I lead

With her, keep the kettle warm
Whistling and on the stove
Never grow up, never leave

Reversed roles take a toll
Leaving me omniscient
and shamefully melancholic

Consorted

Golden and hazel
Yearning for attention and approval
Saying yes to everything and giving my all
It didn't bother me that her leaves were turning brown
Nothing could ever happen with crab apple buds

Drowning and then coming up for air
Yearning for sanity and love
Inflicted over and over, swallowing my pride
It bothered me that I was subaqueous once more
Air moved to greener pastures

A magnetic abduction
Yearning for adventure and novelty
Maternal instincts and stability, lustful
The sting still bothers me
Fairytales are for children, not men

777 on a slot machine, it was rare
Soft voice, skin, nature, and prose
The fire burning within me turned
into a positive, warm hug that I never want to end.

Bridal Chorus

She can't wear white
Nor can she keep black
Roses will have the sharp
violent thorns in your side

Clouds take form faster
than any thoughts of you
Nature takes course
and sand fills the gaps

I do not dream of those
pearls, cakes, and doves..
But when the vows are said,
I know I was the one loved.

To The Place I Belong

Cold.
A simple word to describe you
But it doesn't do you justice.

It's not the only reason I left,
But it's the excuse that comes to mind first.
How I thank God to have seen you in Autumn.

I've seen you in all your seasons, but
I felt your coldness in my bones.
You messed with my mind.

I thought I was far more special,
But I knew I wasn't when I left you.
There was an unknown vastness to explore.

I still buy your syrup, cheeses, and ice cream.
I will always call you home, a safety net.
When the bombs descend, I'm running to you.

Your neighbors will protect us, women and children.
For when the righteous and wrong erupt,
You will always be on the right side of history.

How lucky am I to have climbed your peaks
Slept in your branches, fields, and valleys
But most of all, be a native to your land.

Dancing is a Dangerous Game

A noose, a gun, a drug
These methods just won't do
They've grown tired and untrustworthy
Fearless and unwavering,
Perspective shape shifts from
an apathetic ending to a joyful beginning
Come, hold my hand
Trees can't grow without water
Rain is abundant,
but the light is gone
Days, weeks, months have passed
but do not find solace in my soul's journey
If I make it out, let these wings
grow wide and white
And may I ignore the devil,
when he offers me his hand to dance.

Missing Gratitude

Reliable, I would go anywhere
And do anything, happily volunteering
You could count on me

Stable, surrounded by chaos
I showed you peace and grounded you
Reversing years of doddery

Calm, I made you feel safe
Secure, at home in my arms,
I could quiet your mind

And still,
I became an empty nester
to the grown and unfaithful

Sleepless Nights

The friction is palpable
pulling stray hairs and lint
and the soreness around
my wide eyes swell
Neither side is cool, nor warm, it's
just there, and a basement
to the ringing in my ears.

Recession

It's not the same.
Still no housing or
real money to lose

But the option to grow old
was just that, and at least
I had my gaming console

Now your children can
play 100-pin bowling
while your stocks plummet.

My Turn

I am not a grief counselor, or
a therapist, or a mother
But I've been all three

  It's exhausting.

I've also sat on many couches
In many waiting rooms,
But I was never a child.

Cursed

I wasn't expecting this to last
It's not a blessing to love this deeply
Because the pain of losing what you love
Outweighs and outlasts

Logically, I'm there. The slate is clean.
But one piece of familiarity
Brings me back to day one, and
I want nothing more than to forget.

Even worse is knowing that you have–
Forgotten, or maybe you were never
in that deep to begin with.

I'm just one of hundreds to you,
But I will never have a hundred to hold.

The Climax

Writing in a journal isn't going to help me.
Changing jobs won't fix me.
Learning to accept things isn't a cure.
I have done my part, and there is no
more waiting for you to do yours.

Anywhere but here

Constant need to be
doing something -
Bigger, greater, better

Write a book, take a course
Go back to school or
get a second and third job

No television is watched and
no meal is consumed
without a written review

When you can't succumb to
the fatigue as desired,
you learn to exhaust daylight

Authenticity

The sun came up
and crowds cheered

Always told I'll be better
off, an old soul

Tortured, it may be
But no regrets to be had

Clementine

Looking for a sign
and placing power on
the small, orange fruit

Subconsciously picked
because it's easy to peel
and a beloved hybrid

Dare the fruit to be bitten
and the loss to be forgotten.
Stay little clementine, stay.

Abundance

It pours in, sitting in a pool at the bottom of my stomach
Enlightenment skyrockets,
and the higher self appears as frequently as angel numbers.
So much time has been wasted on my fears
of the cards that I've been dealt.
The destiny is not manifested; it's here.
In my control and my responsibility
It cannot be measured, and I will not worry about paper.
Conspiring streams and watching it all unravel.

Somebody to Love

Soft, warm skin that only responds to my touch
Eyes that flicker between the sun and my mouth
A parcel of love, kindness, strength, and depth.

Magnetism and mystery that knows no bounds
Wealth in places here and people around there
Passion for life, adventure, growth, and health.

You're out there waiting for me, and I know it.
I never had to question you or us for a moment.

Eyes Don't Lie

Maybe it was luck?
Or fate, or planned, or baited
like a worm on a reel, and
that would make sense as to why
I'm as cautious as the fish.

Certainty was not present
but you were. Fully present.
The dish on the wood was far
less appetizing to you in that
moment, when you swallowed me whole.

Was I a fish on a hook, or
was I prey to a predator?
Only time will tell which
unfortunate animal that I am.
I sure hope that I'm not holding the reel.

Let it Be

Let it be. You're not going to be a politician.
No one can hear you. They listen, but they
follow with empty promises and performances.

Let it be. You're not going to understand.
No one will understand you. They will try,
but they have made up their minds and opinions.

Let it be. You're not going to change the world.
No one person can do that. They hope, but they
are in a sea of thousands and ruled by a drop of a dozen.

Let it be. You're going to live this life and be
thankful that you have the one that you do.

Ending the Cycle

I'll never understand how unfair life can be.
My mother has shown me how awful things
happen to the purest of souls with the
hardest working, most loving, and courageous spirits.

My father has shown me how awful things can be, too.
How the color of your skin or the history of your
family can tear you apart and leave you alone to die.

My siblings have shown me how peace comes at a cost
and how intimacy and proximity come with fear.
I will show them all how I can be.

Dominique Sweat

Captured by Catherine Holmes Photography

Dominique was born and raised in the state of Vermont. Growing up in a predominantly White area, she often felt an immense pressure to fit in with those around her. She grew to embrace her ethnicity and appreciate her differences. This wasn't an easy journey as she struggled with her identity, sexuality, and overall purpose in life. After learning from many challenges and experiences, it only felt natural for her to express her efforts to exist through poetry.

www.ingramcontent.com/pod-product-compliance
Lightning Source LLC
Chambersburg PA
CBHW070638130626
46555CB00006B/2607